Introducing Continents

Europe

Chris Oxlade

Heinemann
LIBRARY

Chicago, Illinois

© 2014 Heinemann Library
an imprint of Capstone Global Library, LLC
Chicago, Illinois

To contact Capstone Global Library please phone 800-747-4992, or visit our web site, www.capstonepub.com

Edited by Dan Nunn, Rebecca Rissman, Sian Smith, and Helen Cox Cannons
Designed by Philippa Jenkins
Original illustrations © Capstone Global Library Ltd 2014
Picture research by Liz Alexander and Tristan Leverett
Production by Vicki Fitzgerald
Originated by Capstone Global Library Ltd
Printed and bound in China by Leo Paper Products Ltd

17 16 15 14 13
10 9 8 7 6 5 4 3 2 1

Library of Congress Cataloging-in-Publication Data
Oxlade, Chris.
  Introducing Europe / Chris Oxlade.
      pages cm.—(Introducing continents)
  Includes bibliographical references and index.
  ISBN 978-1-4329-8042-9 (hb)—ISBN 978-1-4329-8050-4 (pb) 1. Europe—Juvenile literature. I. Title.

D1051.O95 2013
940—dc23   2012049495

Acknowledgments
The author and publisher are grateful to the following for permission to reproduce copyright material: Alamy p. 19 (© Eye Ubiquitous); Getty Images pp. 16 (Flickr/Rob Kints), 18 (John Howard/Riser), 26 (Mark A Leman/Stone); naturepl.com p. 14 (© Tom Mangelsen); Shutterstock pp. 6 (© Maugli), 7 (© Bill Poon), 8 (© Prometheus72), 9 (© Johann Helgason), 11 (© Vladimir Mucibabic), 12 (© Wild Arctic Pictures), 13 (© tovovan), 15 (© FotoVeto), 17 (© Foodpictures), 20 (© chantal de bruijne), 21 (© Sergey Petrov), 23 (© AND Inc.), 24 (© Anastasios71), 25 (© Kletr), 27 (© Natalia Mikhaylova); SuperStock p. 10 (Axiom Photographic Limited).

Cover photographs of a beautiful lake in the Danube Delta, Romania and a shaded relief map of Europe reproduced with permission of Shutterstock (© Porojnicu Stelian, © Vitoriano Jr.); image of a cafe at the market square of Greifswald, Germany reproduced with permission of SuperStock (© F1 ONLINE).

Every effort has been made to contact copyright holders of any material reproduced in this book. Any omissions will be rectified in subsequent printings if notice is given to the publisher.

Contents

Some words are shown in bold, **like this**. You can find out what they mean by looking in the glossary.

About Europe

Europe is one of the world's seven **continents**. A continent is a huge area of land. Europe is the second smallest of the continents. The eastern side of Europe is connected to Asia, the largest continent.

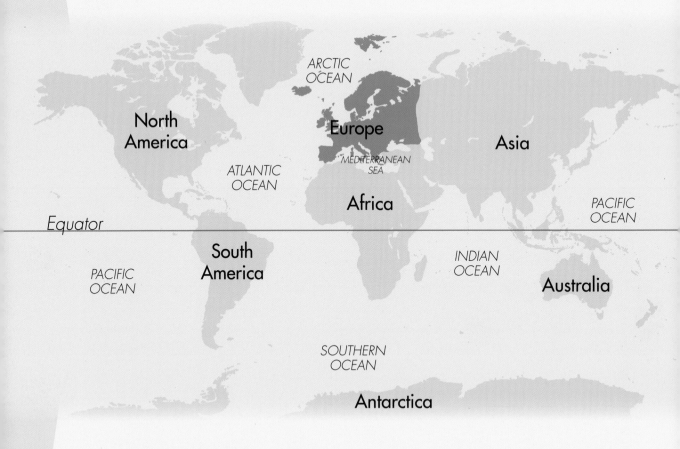

ARCTIC OCEAN

North America

Europe

Asia

ATLANTIC OCEAN

MEDITERRANEAN SEA

Africa

PACIFIC OCEAN

Equator

PACIFIC OCEAN

South America

INDIAN OCEAN

Australia

SOUTHERN OCEAN

Antarctica

The Atlantic Ocean lies to the west of Europe. The Mediterranean Sea lies to the south. To the north is the Arctic Ocean. There are many islands in these oceans that are part of Europe.

Europe Fact File	
Area	3,837,081 square miles (9,938,000 square kilometers)
Population	740 million
Number of countries	49
Highest mountain	Mount Elbrus at 18,510 feet (5,642 meters)
Longest river	Volga River at 2,229 miles (3,700 kilometers)

Famous Places

There are many famous places in Europe. The Colosseum in Rome, Italy, is a huge **arena** that was built almost 2,000 years ago. Romans went to the Colosseum to see gladiators fight each other.

The Colosseum is one of the most popular places to visit in Europe.

The Eiffel Tower is 1,063 feet (324 meters) tall.

The Eiffel Tower is the most famous building in Paris, France. Millions of people go to the top every year. Buckingham Palace in London and Red Square in Moscow, Russia, are other famous places to visit.

Geography

There are many **mountain ranges** in Europe. The Alps are more than 700 miles (1,126 kilometers) long. They stretch from France to Austria. Europe's highest mountain is Mount Elbrus in the Caucasus Mountains.

Mont Blanc is the highest mountain in the Alps.

Ural Mountains

Cantabrian Mountains

Pyrenees

Mont Blanc

Alps

Carpathian Mountains

Caucasus Mountains

Mount Elbrus

0   250 miles
0   400 km

There are some **active volcanoes** in Europe. Mount Etna is on the island of Sicily, in Italy. It erupts every few years. There are more than 30 active volcanoes in Iceland. There are also hot springs and **geysers**.

The Volga is the longest river in Europe. The Rhine and the Danube flow through the middle of Europe. Ships carry **cargo** between cities on these rivers. The Danube flows through nine different countries.

The Danube River flows through Budapest in Hungary.

Lake Onega
Lake Ladoga
Lake Peipus
Lake Vänern
Lake Vättern
Lake Geneva
Lake Lucerne
Lake Balaton

0   250 miles
0   400 km

Europe p8

Chillon castle stands on the shores of Lake Geneva in Switzerland.

Europe has many large lakes. Lake Ladoga in Russia is the largest lake. It is 136 miles (219 kilometers) across. There are beautiful lakes in the mountains of Switzerland and Italy. Finland has thousands of lakes.

Weather

Europe has many different types of weather. In the far north, it is always cold and icy. It is so cold that the ocean is frozen solid. Even in the middle of summer the temperature is only just above freezing.

Snow and ice cover the far north of Europe.

Around the Mediterranean Sea in the south of Europe, the weather is hot and sunny in summer. In most of Europe, summer is warm and winter is cool. It can be rainy at any time of year.

Animals

Polar bears, seals, and reindeer live in the cold **Arctic** parts of Europe. Wolves, bears, deer, and foxes are some of the animals that live in the huge forests in the north of Europe.

Arctic foxes grow a thick, white coat in winter.

The great spotted woodpecker lives in Europe's woodlands.

Golden eagles fly in Europe's hills and mountains. Beautiful flamingos, pelicans, and many other types of birds live in the **delta** of the Danube River. Otters live in rivers, lakes, and along the coast.

Plants and Other Living Things

In the far north of Europe, mosses and **lichens** grow on the frozen **tundra**. There are also forests of conifer trees, such as pine trees and fir trees. Farther south are forests of **deciduous** trees, such as oaks and beeches.

These snow-covered forests are in the far north of Europe.

These olive trees are growing on a farm in Turkey.

Different types of plants grow in the far south, where the weather is warmer and drier. There are olive trees, lemon trees, and orange trees. There are also vineyards full of grape vines.

People

About 738 million people live in Europe. There are many different groups of people, such as Russians, Turks, and Finns. Millions of people from the world's other **continents** live in Europe too.

People from different parts of the world mix together in European cities.

BAYONNE -BAIONA

i P CENTRE VILLE
HIRI BARNEA
Hôtel de Ville -Herriko Etxea
Police -Polizategia

Chapelle Impériale

PLAGES - HONDARTZAK

Most countries in Europe have their own language. In some countries, different groups of people speak different languages. People in Switzerland speak German, French, or Italian.

19

Culture

Soccer is the most popular sport in Europe. Millions of people play it themselves or watch teams such as Manchester City, AC Milan, or Real Madrid. Cycling, rugby, and handball are also very popular.

The Tour de France is the world's most famous cycle race.

These ballet dancers are on stage at the famous Bolshoi Theatre in Moscow.

There are many famous art galleries in Europe, including the Louvre in Paris, France, and the Uffizi Gallery in Florence, Italy. Visitors can see beautiful paintings and sculptures. There are also many famous theaters and opera houses.

Countries

Altogether there are 49 countries in Europe. Russia is easily the largest country, even though only part of Russia is in Europe. The rest is in Asia. The Vatican City in Rome is the smallest country. It is also the smallest country in the world.

This map shows the countries of Europe.

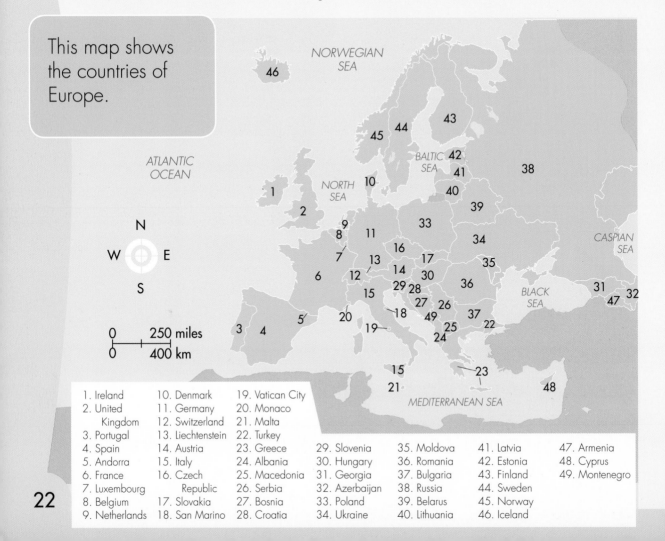

1. Ireland	10. Denmark	19. Vatican City
2. United Kingdom	11. Germany	20. Monaco
3. Portugal	12. Switzerland	21. Malta
4. Spain	13. Liechtenstein	22. Turkey
5. Andorra	14. Austria	23. Greece
6. France	15. Italy	24. Albania
7. Luxembourg	16. Czech Republic	25. Macedonia
8. Belgium	17. Slovakia	26. Serbia
9. Netherlands	18. San Marino	27. Bosnia
		28. Croatia

29. Slovenia	35. Moldova	41. Latvia	47. Armenia
30. Hungary	36. Romania	42. Estonia	48. Cyprus
31. Georgia	37. Bulgaria	43. Finland	49. Montenegro
32. Azerbaijan	38. Russia	44. Sweden	
33. Poland	39. Belarus	45. Norway	
34. Ukraine	40. Lithuania	46. Iceland	

The European Parliament building is in the city of Strasbourg, France.

Twenty-seven countries in Europe are members of a group called the European Union (EU). The countries work together to help each other. The European Union makes laws that must be followed in the different countries.

Cities and Countryside

There are many big cities in Europe. London, Moscow, and Paris are three of the biggest. They are the capital cities of the United Kingdom, Russia, and France. Only one half of the city of Istanbul, in Turkey, is in Europe. The other half is in Asia.

There are ancient buildings in Athens, the capital city of Greece.

Wheat is harvested at the end of the summer.

In the countryside, farmers grow crops and raise animals such as cattle, sheep, and pigs. Wheat is the most common crop. It is used to make bread and pasta. In the far north of Europe, it is too cold to grow crops.

Natural Resources and Products

Europe has many **natural resources**. Wood is harvested from the forests of northern Europe. New trees are planted to replace the ones that are cut down. Coal is an important fuel. It is dug from the ground in Russia, Germany, and Poland.

This oil rig in the North Sea pumps oil from under the seabed.

Models show off the latest fashions on the runway during London Fashion Week.

There are many car-making factories in Europe. Famous makes of cars made there are Volkswagen, BMW, and Audi. There is also a big fashion industry. Fashion shows take place in Paris, Milan, and London.

Fun Facts

- The Caspian Sea is the world's biggest lake, but it is called a sea because it is full of salt water.

- The coast of Norway has many deep valleys filled by seawater that reach far inland. They are called fjords (say "fee-yords").

- Venice is a city in Italy that is built on islands. There are canals instead of streets, and people travel around by boat.

- In some parts of the Netherlands, the land is below the level of the sea. The water is held back by giant banks and dams.

Quiz

1. Which is the longest river in Russia?

2. Which two countries are half in Europe and half in Asia?

3. What is Etna? And where is it?

4. What is the most popular sport in Europe?

4. Soccer

3. It's a volcano, on the island of Sicily in Italy

2. Russia and Turkey

1. The Volga

Glossary

active volcano mountain with a hole in the top that ash or hot melted rock comes out of

Arctic area of Earth around the North Pole, where it is always cold

arena building where sports events and other events are held

cargo anything carried by a ship, truck, or plane, such as coal, oil, stone, or goods such as cars, fridges, or computers

continent one of seven huge areas of land on Earth

deciduous tree that loses its leaves in winter

delta area shaped like a triangle where a river splits and flows into a sea or ocean

geyser natural fountain of hot water and steam, made by hot rocks under the ground

lichen simple plants that grow on the bark of trees, on rock, and on walls

mountain range large group of mountains

natural resources natural materials that we use, such as wood, coal, oil, and rock

tundra large area of flat land with no trees near the Arctic

Find Out More

Books

Bingham, Jane. *Exploring Europe*. Chicago: Heinemann, 2007.

Gibson, Karen Bush. *Spotlight on Europe*. Mankato, Minn.: Capstone, 2011.

Royston, Angela and Michael Scott. *Europe's Most Amazing Plants*. Chicago: Raintree, 2009.

Websites

FactHound offers a safe, fun way to find Internet sites related to this book. All of the sites on FactHound have been researched by our staff.

Here's all you do:
Visit www.facthound.com
Type in this code: 9781432980429

Index